NATIONAL GEOGRAPHIC

# Birds

Stewart Gardiner

Some birds are big.

Some birds are small.

Some birds are black.

Some birds are yellow.

Some birds can fly.

Some birds can swim.

These birds are different, but all birds are alike in some ways.

How are all birds the same?

All birds hatch from eggs.

All birds have feathers.

All birds have a beak.

All birds have two legs.

What else do all birds have?

Wings!